Original title:
Summer's Splendid Song

Copyright © 2024 Creative Arts Management OÜ
All rights reserved.

Author: Thor Castlebury
ISBN HARDBACK: 978-9916-85-786-1
ISBN PAPERBACK: 978-9916-85-787-8

Laughter in the Heat of Day

In the swelter of the afternoon glow,
Children's laughter dances, breezes flow,
Sunlight spills like honey on the ground,
In moments of joy, pure bliss is found.

Shadows stretch long beneath the trees,
Where whispers of laughter ride on the breeze,
In echoes of play, the world fades away,
Under the sun, worries hold no sway.

The Canvas of Azure Dreams

Beneath the skies where whispers unfold,
A canvas of azure, bright and bold,
Brush strokes of clouds weave stories above,
Painting the heavens with hues of love.

Stars twinkle softly in twilight's embrace,
Each dream a constellation, a precious trace,
In this vast expanse, our hopes take flight,
A tapestry woven of day and night.

Days Adorned with Nature's Jewels

Mornings greet with dewdrops bright,
Nature's jewels in the soft sunlight,
Blossoms open, fluttering with grace,
A symphony of colors fills the space.

Amidst the leaves, whispers of the breeze,
Life's vibrant palette, the heart's sweet ease,
Each moment a treasure, wild and free,
In the embrace of nature, we find harmony.

A Symphony in the Garden

In the garden where melodies play,
Flowers sway gently, night turns to day,
A symphony blossoms, soft and serene,
Nature orchestrates a vibrant scene.

Birds chirp sweetly, notes fill the air,
While rustling leaves weave a tune so rare,
Each petal a note in this living score,
In a garden's embrace, we long for more.

Nightfall's Velvet Embrace

As twilight drapes in shades of blue,
The stars unfold their wishes bright,
Whispers of dreams in the cool night dew,
Cradled in the arms of soft moonlight.

Silhouettes dance where shadows play,
In gardens where the night blooms thrive,
The world rests gently, in nature's ballet,
Awakening souls in the hush of the skies.

Chasing Light Against the Horizon

With every dawn, the chase begins,
A canvas spreads where colors collide,
The sun arises, shedding its sins,
Soft rays weaving, a warm, golden tide.

Through valleys deep and mountains high,
We follow trails where daylight spills,
With hopes that stretch and dreams that fly,
Igniting hearts with spirited thrills.

Reflections in the Glimmering Lake

Upon the lake, the mirror glows,
A tranquil surface, crystal clear,
Whispers of nature, secrets it knows,
Emotions dance in the atmosphere.

The willows lean with gentle grace,
Their shadows ripple, soft caress,
In this stillness, we find our place,
Lost in reverie, in silence, we bless.

Vibrant Hues of Nature's Paintbrush

With every stroke, the earth awakes,
In hues of amber, violet, green,
A symphony that nature makes,
In every corner, beauty is seen.

Flowers bloom like laughter's song,
Underneath the nurturing sun,
A gallery where we all belong,
In nature's arms, we are one.

Flickers of Fireflies and Wishes

In the garden's gentle whisper, they dance,
Flickers of fireflies weaving dreams of chance,
Softly glowing orbs, in twilight's warm glow,
Each spark a wish, where hopes and moments flow.

Underneath the starry quilt, secrets they keep,
Their light guides the heart, in the night so deep,
A symphony of wishes, on a summer breeze,
Carried by the nightingale, through rustling trees.

Twilight's Soft Embrace

As the sun dips low, painting skies with grace,
Twilight unfolds, a tender, warm embrace,
Shadows stretch long, while whispers softly blend,
Time sways gently, as day begins to end.

Stars peep out shyly, twinkling in their flight,
Bathed in the moon's glow, the world feels just right,
Crickets serenade, in hushed melodic tune,
Wrapped in twilight's hush, cradled by the moon.

The Joyride of Endless Green

In fields of emerald, where dreams take flight,
Joyrides of laughter, in the morning light,
Each blade of grass sways in rhythmic delight,
A tapestry woven, of day and night.

With every step taken, innocence found,
The scent of wildflowers, fragrant and profound,
Nature's embrace, so vast and serene,
A canvas of earth, where all hearts convene.

A Mosaic of Sun-drenched Memories

In the amber glow of a sun drenched day,
Memories radiate, in a vibrant display,
Laughter echoes wide, like waves on the shore,
Each moment a brushstroke, in life's endless lore.

Captured in photographs, smiles frozen in time,
A mosaic of colors, a beautiful rhyme,
From sunlit adventures to whispers of peace,
In the heart's gallery, where all joys increase.

Crystal Waters

Beneath the surface, secrets lie,
Where shimmering depths reflect the sky.
The dance of ripples in the sun's warm embrace,
Whispers of dreams in this tranquil place.

A world awakened with every tide,
Soft echoes echo where shadows abide.
Life spirals gently in crystal's refrain,
Where joy finds solace and sorrow's arcane.

Whispered Wishes

In twilight's hush, the stars ignite,
Cradled in the arms of the night.
With every breath, a wish takes flight,
On silver streams of soft moonlight.

In gentle murmurs, hopes entwine,
Each quiet call, a sacred sign.
Chasing the shadows, they'll surely find,
The promise of dreams, tender and kind.

Euphoria in a Gentle Breeze

With every gust, the blossoms sway,
In fields of gold where the wild hearts lay.
A scent of freedom, a taste of grace,
In the caress of air, we find our place.

The whispering leaves in symphony play,
Turning grey skies to a canvas of day.
Euphoria dances on the wind's embrace,
In nature's arms, we find our pace.

The Heartbeat of a Season

In winter's chill, when the world goes still,
The heartbeat echoes, a rhythmic thrill.
Spring's tender bloom is a soft refrain,
As life awakens from frost's gentle chain.

Summer's laughter fills sun-drenched skies,
While autumn's colors begin to rise.
Each season whispers its own sweet song,
In nature's cycle, we all belong.

Carousel of Color and Light

A whirl of hues in the evening glow,
Spinning in circles where dreams overflow.
The canvas spins, a bright serenade,
With each stroke of brush, new worlds are made.

In vibrant laughter, the colors play,
A carousel turning both night and day.
We ride the rhythm, lost in delight,
On this journey of color and light.

Joys of the Garden Gala

In vibrant hues the petals sway,
A dance of colors in the light of day.
Bees hum softly, their work divine,
As nature sings in a perfect line.

With laughter ringing, children play,
Amidst the blooms where dreams stay.
Each blossom tells a tale anew,
In the garden's arms, the heart breaks through.

Basking in Nature's Warm Embrace

Beneath the branches, shadows blend,
Where whispers of the forest send
A gentle kiss from earth to sky,
Inviting all to linger nigh.

The sun cascades in golden streams,
Awakening the wildest dreams.
In every leaf and rustling sound,
A symphony of peace is found.

Golden Days and Sunlit Rays

Time drips slowly in the afternoon,
As laughter dances like a sweet tune.
Barefoot moments on the grass,
In golden light, our troubles pass.

Each ray a brushstroke, soft and fair,
Painting smiles on faces bare.
In this fleeting, blissful gaze,
We cherish life in golden days.

The Melody of Warm Breezes

The breeze sings softly through the trees,
Carrying tales on whispers of ease.
With every gust, the world feels free,
A harmony of earth and sea.

Under the sky, we close our eyes,
Listening to nature's lullabies.
In every sigh, the heart finds peace,
A melody that will never cease.

Whispers of Warmth

In the soft glow of the early dawn,
Gentle whispers caress the air,
Embracing hearts with a tender song,
As sunlight weaves through strands of care.

Each leaf trembles with stories untold,
Wrapped in the warmth of nature's embrace,
The world awakens from dreams of gold,
As joy radiates in every space.

The Dance of Sunlight

Sunlight twirls on the edge of the lake,
Like laughter ringing in summer's embrace,
Ripples of joy in each shimmer and shake,
A radiant waltz in this tranquil place.

The trees stretch their limbs, inviting a kiss,
While shadows perform in a play of delight,
Nature's own chorus, a moment of bliss,
As day transforms softly into the night.

Blooms in the Breeze

Petals flutter like whispers on air,
In gardens where secrets and colors collide,
Each blossom's laughter a promise to share,
In nature's mosaic, her beauty abides.

The breeze carries tales of the life that it wakes,
With each graceful sway, and each fragrant sigh,
Nature's canvas, in hues it remakes,
Takes flight on the wings of a jubilant sky.

Golden Hours Unraveled

As daylight spills gold on the horizon wide,
Moments awaken, in warmth they swell,
A tapestry rich, where solace resides,
In the heart's quiet corner, time weaves its spell.

Each tick of the clock whispers sweetly of dreams,
Where echoes of laughter and love intertwine,
In the golden embrace of soft twilight beams,
Life dances in rhythm, where memories shine.

Songs of the Sweltering Sun

Beneath the blazing, golden sphere,
The earth submits to sultry sway,
With every ray, a story clear,
Of summer's fervent, timeless play.

The cicadas sing their fervent tune,
While shadows stretch and wane and bend,
Each heartbeat sipping June's warm moon,
As daylight dances without end.

The breeze, a whispering, warm embrace,
Caresses skin, so soft and warm,
While sun-kissed laughter fills the space,
In nature's wild and vibrant charm.

Oh, songs of sun, both bold and bright,
In your embrace, we lose all care,
With hearts aglow in the golden light,
We find our rhythm in the air.

Evening's Gentle Whisper

As twilight drapes the world in hues,
A palette rich of softest grace,
The sky exhales a breath of blues,
While stars prepare to take their place.

The trees stand tall with secrets kept,
In shadows deep, old stories sigh,
While crickets weave the dreams we've slept,
As echoes of the day drift by.

A fleeting breeze, so tender, mild,
Caresses cheeks like whispered prayers,
In this still hour, the world, beguiled,
Awakens hopes and softens cares.

Evening speaks in hushed refrain,
As night unveils its velvet hand,
In quietude, we find our gain,
In the embrace of twilight's band.

Fragrance of Petals and Possibility

In gardens where the blossoms bloom,
The air is thick with sweet delight,
Each petal whispers of its plume,
A tale of dreams wrapped in the night.

The roses blush with fervent dreams,
While lilies dance in morning's dew,
With every scent, the heart redeems,
A hint of hope, a love anew.

The dappled sun through leaves does play,
Creating paths of light and shade,
In fragrant winds, we find the way,
To seek the paths our hearts have made.

A flower's grace in scented air,
Invites us to explore and feel,
For in each bloom, a world to share,
Fragrance of life, a vivid reel.

Gentle Laughter in the Air

In fields where children laugh and run,
The sun doth cast its golden spell,
Each giggle echoes, purest fun,
A symphony of joy to tell.

The daisies sway to softest tunes,
While dreams take flight on whispered wings,
With every burst, our spirit croons,
As laughter dances, sweetly sings.

The world alive with mirth and light,
Their innocence, a treasure rare,
In every glance, pure delight,
Creating bonds in the fresh air.

So let us bask in laughs we share,
In this embrace of childlike grace,
For in such moments, free from care,
We find our hearts in joyous space.

Frolic in the Fields

In fields of gold where daisies sway,
The laughter of children brightens the day.
Kites dance high on a gentle breeze,
Nature's symphony sings through the trees.

With each step through the wildflowers' maze,
We twirl and spin in a sunlit haze.
Joy spills forth like a bubbling stream,
In this Eden, we dance, we dream.

Twilight's Gentle Caress

As the sun dips low and shadows play,
Twilight wraps the world in a warm display.
Stars begin to twinkle in the dusky light,
The moon whispers secrets to the coming night.

Soft hues blend into the velvet sky,
Crickets whisper in a lullaby.
Each moment lingers, sweet and sublime,
In twilight's embrace, we find our rhyme.

Beneath the Boughs of Abundance

Beneath the boughs where the ripe fruits gleam,
Whispers of nature weave a silent dream.
The air is rich with the scent of earth,
Here lies the hush of life, and its worth.

Branches cradle a bounty so grand,
We gather close in this fruitful land.
Hands meet the harvest, a shared delight,
Beneath the boughs, our hearts take flight.

Frosted Lemonade and Laughter

On a summer's day, with the sun aglow,
We sip frosted lemonade, feeling the flow.
Laughter dances on the tongue like sweet,
In this moment of joy, life tastes complete.

Friends gather 'round, the chatter is free,
Memories poured like sugar in tea.
Each sip a reminder of warmth and cheer,
In frosted delights, our hearts draw near.

Fields of Gold and Green

In the fields of gold and green, we dance,
Underneath the sun's warm glance.
Whispers of the breeze so fine,
Nature's beauty, pure design.

Golden grains that sway with grace,
A tapestry that time won't erase.
Beneath the sky, so vast and wide,
In this paradise, we take our stride.

The sun dips low, a fiery sphere,
Casting shadows, drawing near.
With every rustle, a story told,
In these fields of magic, we behold.

So let us roam 'neath endless skies,
With laughter echoing, spirits rise.
In the fields where dreams convene,
Life's a treasure, gold and green.

Lullabies of the Lazy Afternoon

In the cradle of the afternoon light,
Whispers of dreams take gentle flight.
Softly woven through sunbeams' glow,
Lullabies of comfort, sweet and slow.

With every rustle of leaves above,
Nature sings a song of love.
The world slows down, in peaceful bliss,
Wrapped in warmth, a tender kiss.

Time drifts like clouds, so carefree,
Beneath the shade of the old oak tree.
In a symphony of sighs and starts,
Lazy afternoons tug at our hearts.

So let us dream beneath the sun,
In this tranquil place, we are one.
The world awaits, but here we'll stay,
With lullabies to guide our play.

Flavors of Freedom and Fun

Beneath the suns of laughter and cheer,
Adventure calls, the moment is near.
With every flavor, wild and bright,
We taste the essence of pure delight.

From juicy fruits to spicy delights,
Crisp, sweet echoes of summer nights.
Each bite a story of wandering feet,
In the dance of flavors, we find our beat.

With open skies and hearts ablaze,
We savor life in a joyous haze.
Freedom flows in every shared bite,
Together we shine, vibrant and bright.

So come, let's dive into the feast,
Explore the flavors, the fun, the least.
In this celebration of all things spun,
We find our joy, our freedom, our fun.

Cherished Moments in Bloom

In gardens where the wildflowers sway,
Moments captured, come what may.
Every petal whispers secrets divine,
In cherished blooms, our hearts entwine.

With colors bursting, a painter's dream,
Each blossom a memory, pure as cream.
Bees hum softly, the sun shines bright,
Life blooms anew in radiant light.

Time lingers gently on petals soft,
In the dance of flowers, our spirits loft.
Hand in hand, we wander free,
In this fragrant world, just you and me.

So let us savor the fleeting hours,
In cherished moments, we find our powers.
As seasons change, our love will bloom,
Forever cherished, dispelling the gloom.

Radiance of the Season

Golden hues embrace the trees,
Leaves dance lightly in the breeze,
Sunlight streams through branches high,
Awakening dreams beneath the sky.

Fields adorned in vibrant gold,
Whispers of warmth, a tale retold,
Nature dons her finest gown,
In this brilliance, we won't drown.

Blossoms Beneath the Blue

Petals blush in the morning light,
Beneath the blue, they take to flight,
A symphony of scents in the air,
Each blossom a joy, beyond compare.

Streaks of lavender and softest pink,
In a world of color, together we sync,
Time stands still as we breathe it in,
Life's fleeting beauty, where love begins.

Joyride through Wildflowers

Wanderlust guides our eager feet,
Through fields where the earth and heaven meet,
A tapestry woven with colors bright,
In wildflowers' embrace, our spirits take flight.

Laughter mingles with the buzzing bees,
As we chase the whisper of the breeze,
Hand in hand through nature's delight,
In this joyful ride, hearts feel so light.

The Canvas of Twilight

As day concedes to soothing night,
The sky transforms in fading light,
Brushstrokes of amber and deepening blue,
A masterpiece born anew.

Crickets serenade the quiet ground,
In this gentle hush, peace is found,
Stars awaken, one by one,
In the canvas of twilight, our dreams run.

Embrace of the Endless Sky

Beneath the vast expanse where dreams take flight,
Clouds dance and swirl, a canvas of pure delight.
Whispers of the wind echo soft and low,
In the embrace of the endless sky, time feels like slow.

Stars begin to twinkle in twilight's sweet glow,
As twilight bids farewell, two hearts start to flow.

In each hue of blue, a story unfolds,
In the embrace of the endless sky, love's warmth never gets old.

A Serenade for Sun-Kissed Souls

In a meadow where laughter and wildflowers align,
Sunlight drapes softly, a shimmering line.
The breeze carries secrets of love intertwined,
A serenade for sun-kissed souls, beautifully designed.

With each gentle note, the world finds its tune,
As shadows dance lightly beneath the bright moon.
Hearts in unison, as one they become,
In a serenade for sun-kissed souls, forever hum.

Sunlight Through the Canopy

In the forest deep where ancient trees sigh,
Sunlight filters gently, a soft lullaby.
Golden beams painting the ground with such grace,
Sunlight through the canopy, a sacred embrace.

With each rustling leaf, a whispering tale,
Of moments shared softly, like a gentle sail.
Life dances in shadows, a twinkling delight,
Sunlight through the canopy, nature's pure light.

Colors of a Lazy Afternoon

Draped in cotton clouds, the world moves in slow,

Golden rays shimmer where the soft breezes blow.
With each passing moment, colors begin to blend,

In the tapestry of life, where time seems to suspend.

Pastel skies mingle with laughter and dreams,
Captured in the warmth of sun-kissed beams.
Each brushstroke of light paints a tranquil scene,
Colors of a lazy afternoon, serene and pristine.

The Music of Midsummer Nights

In twilight's hush, the stars ignite,
Melodies woven, soft and bright.
Crickets serenade the night so clear,
Whispers of love ride on the warm, clement air.

The moon, a muse, in silver attire,
Guides hearts aflame with a gentle fire.
Each note a memory, faint yet bold,
In the symphony of summer, timelessly told.

Vibrant Days in Bloom

With dawn's embrace, the world awakes,
Petals unfurl, as if the earth takes.
Colors collide in a dance so bright,
Nature's artistry, a pure delight.

The bees hum softly, a buzzing song,
While butterflies flit, both graceful and strong.
In radiant fields where laughter flows,
Life's vibrant pulse in each blossom glows.

Lush Gardens and Laughter

In gardens lush and scents divine,
Laughter twirls like ivy on vine.
Children's giggles dance through the trees,
As blossoms sway to a gentle breeze.

Roses blush in hues of desire,
While daisies boast of youthful fire.
Every bloom tells a story sweet,
Of joy found in nature's heartbeat.

Echoes of Sun-Drenched Skies

Under sun-drenched skies, dreams take flight,
With every horizon, the world feels right.
A canvas of blue, kissed by warm glow,
Paints the laughter of children below.

Clouds drift lazily, whispers of soft tales,
While the wind carries secrets on gentle gales.
In the embrace of the day, worries cease,
And hearts find solace, a moment of peace.

Blossoms Beneath the Glorious Sun

In gardens where the petals bloom bright,
Sunlight dances on each delicate hue,
Whispers of spring fill the air with delight,
Nature unveils a wondrous debut.

With every blossom unfurling its grace,
The world awakens from winter's cold hold,
Color spills vibrant through time and through space,
A tapestry woven in stories untold.

Beneath the vast sky, the flowers all sway,
A symphony painted in emerald dreams,
In moments of joy, the heart finds its way,
As life intertwines with sweet sunrays' beams.

Together they flourish, in warmth they abide,
Each petal a promise, each stem a soft sigh,
Under the sun where the secrets reside,
Blossoms bloom boldly, reaching for the sky.

Toes in the Sand, Heart in the Sky

Barefoot on shores where the wild waves play,
Sand cradles dreams in its golden embrace,
The sun bows down with the close of the day,
While seagulls soar high, dancing through space.

Each grain a whisper of stories once told,
The rhythm of tides serenades the soul,
With toes in the sand, I feel rich, I feel bold,
As the sky melts to orange, a sight to console.

The breeze carries laughter, a sweet serenade,
While time lingers softly, a soft lullaby,
In moments like these, all worries fade,
Toes in the sand, heart in the sky.

Under the heavens, a canvas so grand,
I find my own place in this vast, endless sea,
With each crashing wave, I take a firm stand,
In harmony, living, forever free.

Vistas of Endless Blue

Across the horizon where ocean meets air,
Vistas unfold, a breathless embrace,
The azure expanse invites wanderers there,
A canvas of dreams, a vast, open space.

Clouds drift like whispers on a gentle breeze,
Kissing the water with delicate grace,
The sunlight cascades, a golden tease,
Strokes of light paint every crevice and trace.

Mountains on the edge of a wavering line,
Hold secrets of ages in their stout forms,
In the distance, they shimmer, mere shadows divine,
Reflecting the hope of all human storms.

Embraced by the sky, unbound and so true,
In vistas of blue, I am free to explore,
Nature's own promise in every hue,
In the wonders of life, forever I soar.

The Flute of the Wind

Amidst the trees where the wild spirits dwell,
The flute of the wind plays a haunting refrain,
Carving sweet melodies, casting a spell,
A symphony woven in joy and in pain.

It dances through branches, a soft serenade,
Whirling through meadows where wildflowers gleam,
The earth holds its breath as the echoes cascade,
In the heart of the forest, the world loses steam.

With whispers of stories that haven't been heard,
It tells of the stars in the velvety night,
A cosmic connection, each note like a word,
Painting the silence in shadows of light.

So listen, dear soul, to its mystical song,
For life in its essence is ever in flight,
In the flute of the wind, we all can belong,
As it cradles our dreams on the edge of the night.

Whispers of the Sunlit Hours

In the golden glow where shadows play,
The sun spills secrets of the day,
Each ray a whisper, soft and clear,
Inviting hearts to draw near.

Through rustling leaves, the breezes hum,
A symphony sweet where dreams become,
The warmth of moments, fleeting yet bright,
In whispers of the sunlit light.

Dance of the Dappled Light

Beneath the canopy, the light weaves grace,
A dance of shadows in the wild embrace,
Each flicker woven like a lover's sigh,
A tapestry gold against the sky.

The trees sway gently, in perfect time,
As sunbeams twirl, a melody in rhyme,
With every step, the earth takes flight,
In the dance of the dappled light.

Radiant Skies and Gentle Tides

Beneath the arching vault so wide,
The radiant skies and gentle tides,
Whispers of clouds, in a velvet sweep,
Secrets of time in silence keep.

The ocean's song sings sweet and low,
As waves caress the shores we know,
And in the balance, moments reside,
In radiant skies and gentle tides.

Harmonies of Blooming Meadows

In fields where wildflowers joyfully sway,
The harmonies of bloom greet the day,
A canvas of colors, vibrant and free,
Nature's own symphony, called into plea.

Butterflies flit, like notes in the air,
In this fragrant world, all burdens rare,
The heart finds solace, a tranquil abode,
In harmonies of blooming meadows bestowed.

Laughter on the Horizon

In the morning glow, laughter breaks,
A chorus of joy, as dawn awakes,
Echoing softly through valleys wide,
Hope dances freely, nothing to hide.

Every chuckle carries the weight of care,
Floating like whispers in the crisp air,
With each rising sun, the shadows retreat,
Creating a symphony, a world so sweet.

Anthem of the Skylark

Up above the fields, a melody soars,
A skylark sings, as the spirit adores,
With notes that weave through the tender breeze,
Painting the canvas of life with ease.

Through the golden wheat, her song does flow,
Telling tales of love in the sun's warm glow,
A whistle of promise, a heart that reflects,
An anthem of freedom that nature protects.

Tides of Sunlit Dreams

Waves caress the shore with gentle care,
Carrying whispers of dreams laid bare,
Sunlight dances on the water's crest,
Where hopes are cast, and hearts find rest.

Each tide that rises brings stories anew,
Of wanderers' wishes and skies so blue,
In this tranquil embrace of land and sea,
We find reflections of who we can be.

Radiant Days Ahead

As the horizon blushes with light,
We stand on the brink of day turning bright,
With every heartbeat, a spark ignites,
Transforming shadows into new heights.

Together we walk, hand in hand like friends,
Through whispers of promise that summer sends,

The path ahead, radiant and clear,
Invites us to rise, to conquer our fear.

The Spirit of Twilight Melodies

As day retreats, the shadows play,
In hues of purple, gold, and gray,
The whispers call from dusk's embrace,
A serenade of time and space.

Each note a sigh, a gentle breeze,
Stirring the heart among the trees,
The spirit dances, light and bold,
In twilight's grasp, a tale unfolds.

The stars emerge with twinkling eyes,
Awakening secrets of the skies,
A symphony that softly glows,
Where every dream and memory flows.

Tapestry of Heat and Heart

In summer's grip, where passions bloom,
The air is thick with sweet perfume,
Each heartbeat echoes, warm and clear,
Weaving through moments that draw us near.

The sun's embrace ignites the flame,
A vivid dance, unbound by name,
With laughter swirling, like the breeze,
We lose ourselves among the trees.

Each golden ray, a brush of fate,
In this warm world, we celebrate,
The threads of love, so rich, so bright,
A tapestry of day and night.

Soaking Up the Sun's Serenade

On ocean's edge, where waves collide,
The sun spills gold on water wide,
We close our eyes, in warmth, we trust,
Amidst the salt and sun-kissed dust.

Each splash a laugh, each ripple sings,
Of summer's joys and fleeting things,
With footprints drawn in shifting sand,
We dance to time, hand in hand.

From dawn's soft light to twilight's glow,
We savor moments, letting go,
Soaking up the sun's serenade,
Creating memories that won't fade.

Effervescent Evenings

When twilight spills its ruby hues,
The world transforms, and dreams ensue,
A canvas painted with delight,
As day gives way to soft twilight.

The laughter of the stars ignites,
In whispers shared on magical nights,
With candlelight and gentle sighs,
We speak of wonders 'neath the skies.

Each moment sparkles, bright and free,
In effervescent harmony,
For as the moonlight starts to gleam,
We chase the stars, we live the dream.

Fables Written in the Stars

In the canopy where dreams unfold,
Constellations whisper tales of old,
Each star a word on the page of night,
Crafting fables of love, hope, and plight.

Moments captured in celestial ink,
Stories of lives that make us think,
Galaxies dance in a cosmic ballet,
Guiding our hearts along the way.

Wisdom flows in the silence of space,
In every twinkle, a soul finds its place,
For beneath the heavens' endless glow,
Our own small fables continue to grow.

The Pulse of Life Beneath the Shade

Under the boughs where shadows play,
A quiet heartbeat sings through the day,
Whispers of leaves in the dappled light,
Stories of life wrapped in nature's might.

Roots intertwine in a dance below,
Echoing secrets that few come to know,
The pulse of flowers, the sigh of the grass,
Reminding us all of the moments that pass.

In each gentle rustle, a lesson bestowed,
In stillness lies energy waiting to explode,
Here in this haven, time's worries allayed,
Life's simple wonders unfolded in shade.

An Archive of Joyful Echoes

In laughter's embrace, memories reside,
Moments of joy where our hearts collide,
A chorus of smiles that paints the air,
Every echo a treasure, every giggle a prayer.

Sunlight dances on the page of the past,
Fleeting fragments, too beautiful to last,
Yet in our hearts, they find a home,
An archive of joy where we always roam.

Through the trials, through the strife,
These echoes of laughter breathe in our life,
Holding us close with a warm, gentle light,
Guiding our souls through the dark of the night.

Breezes Carrying Fragrance

A soft whisper drifts through the air,
Bringing the scent of blossoms rare,
Carried on winds of a gentle embrace,
Nature's perfume, a delicate lace.

The lilac's sigh, the rose's sweet kiss,
Breezes converge in a fragrant bliss,
Each gust tells stories of gardens in bloom,
Spreading enchantment, dispelling all gloom.

With every inhalation, memories awaken,
Of sun-drenched afternoons, laughter unshaken,
So let the breezes weave through your day,
Carrying fragrance, come what may.

The Warmth of Elysium

In fields where golden sunlight spills,
A gentle breeze the silence fills,
With whispered tones of life anew,
Elysium paints the world in hue.

The laughter of the brook nearby,
Chants melodies that sing and fly,
Upon the wings of fragrant blooms,
And dances past the twilight's glooms.

Each sunset bathes the sky in flame,
A canvas vast, without a name,
Where dreams are woven in the air,
And hope finds solace everywhere.

So linger here, let time be still,
Embrace the warmth, the heart to fill,
In Elysium's embrace so sweet,
Find life, where love and beauty meet.

Melodies of the Meadow

A symphony of rustling leaves,
Where daisies dance and willow weaves,
The whispers of the grass outspread,
Carry secrets yet unsaid.

The brook's soft laughter, bright and clear,
Echoes through the atmosphere,
With every note a story told,
Nature's chorus, pure and bold.

The sunlight spills like liquid gold,
Upon the petals, brave and bold,
Inviting all to take a rest,
In the meadow's heart, forever blessed.

So close your eyes, let rhythms soar,
In this serene and sacred lore,
Where melodies of quiet sway,
Will guide you through the golden day.

Gentle Waves, Sweet Days

The ocean breathes in tides of light,
While seagulls dance in playful flight,
Each wave a whisper, soft and low,
Sings secrets only they can know.

The sun descends, a fiery ray,
As evening draws the end of day,
And every splash, a laugh to share,
In golden moments, hearts laid bare.

Together we embrace the night,
As stars emerge, a twinkling sight,
On soft sand where dreams take form,
Within this gentle, soothing storm.

So let the waves wash fears away,
In tranquil dances, come what may,
For in the ocean's sweet embrace,
We find our quiet, sacred space.

Chasing Fireflies at Dusk

As twilight falls and shadows play,
The world transforms in soft decay,
With whispered dreams, we gather near,
Chasing fireflies, light and dear.

They twinkle bright like stars set free,
Illuminating you and me,
In laughter soft, the night unfolds,
Wrapped in warmth against the cold.

Each flicker captures fleeting time,
A dance of magic, pure, sublime,
In every glow, a memory flashes,
Of summer nights and sweet romances.

So hold this moment in your heart,
As fireflies twirl and never part,
For in their glow, we find our way,
Through chasing dreams at end of day.

The Stillness of a Starry Sky

In the velvet night, the stars align,
Whispers of the cosmos, soft and divine.
A tranquil hush blankets the land,
Holding time in a gentle hand.

Below, the world fades to a dream,
Where starlight shimmers and moonbeams gleam.

Each distant twinkle, a tale untold,
In the silent embrace of the night so bold.

Crickets serenade with their sweet refrain,
While shadows dance in an ethereal chain.
The universe stretches its arms wide and free,
Inviting all souls to find harmony.

As night deepens, the spirit will soar,
Finding peace in the celestial lore.
So let us linger, hearts in the glow,
Lost in the stillness, where dreams always flow.

Glimmering Lagoons and Laughter

In the sun's embrace, the lagoons shimmer bright,

Where laughter dances on waves of pure light.
Beneath palm fronds that sway in soft glee,
Nature's canvas paints joy, wild and free.

Children's giggles cascade like the tide,
As seagulls glide gracefully, side by side.
Echoes of warmth in each splash and play,
Capture the essence of a blissful day.

With each sunset, the colors ignite,
A tapestry woven in crimson and white.
Glimmers of memories flow with the breeze,
Filling the heart with moments that tease.

Together we gather, hand in hand we stand,
Forever enchanted by this sun-kissed land.
In glimmering lagoons where laughter takes flight,
We find our solace, pure and bright.

The Opus of the Ocean

The ocean sings its timeless refrain,
A symphony echoing, wild and unchained.
With every wave crashing, a story is spun,
An opus of life beneath the bold sun.

Tides rise and fall, with a heartbeat so deep,
In its salty embrace, mysteries sleep.
Whales hum their sonnets, while dolphins at play,
Choreograph dances in the light of the day.

Seashells, the notes, collected with care,
Each one a treasure, a moment to share.
The horizon stretches, a canvas so grand,
Where dreams and reality meld into sand.

So let us be carried by this liquid song,
Where oceanic rhythms urge us along.
In the opus of waves, our spirits will soar,
Forever enchanted by that mighty encore.

An Ode to Daydreams

In the quiet hours when shadows shy,
Daydreams flutter like birds on high.
They whisper secrets in the softest light,
Painting our thoughts in colors so bright.

On the edge of reality, we wander and weave,
We find our wishes; we learn to believe.
With every heartbeat, imagination takes flight,
Transforming the mundane to pure delight.

Clouds become castles, the sky an embrace,
In the realm of daydreams, we find our place.
With wings made of wonder, we float through the haze,
In the dance of the moments, we linger and gaze.

So here's to the dreamers, to visions untold,
For in every daydream, we find life's gold.
Embrace the enchantment, let your heart sing,
In the tapestry woven by daydreams, take wing.

Nature's Vibrant Canvas

In the forest where colors collide,
Emerald leaves by the riverside,
Floral hues dance in the breeze,
Nature paints with effortless ease.

Mountains rise with a regal grace,
Clouds embrace the sun's warm face,
Each petal whispers, each branch resounds,
Life's symphony in vibrant bounds.

Every sunset drapes the sky,
Painting moments as time whispers by,
With art that's made of earth and sky,
Nature's hands, the tools they ply.

The world, a canvas set ablaze,
In awe we wander, lost in its maze,
For every scene, a story spun,
In Nature's realm, we find our fun.

The Joy of Sunbeams

Sunbeams dance on morning dew,
Golden hues in skies of blue,
Whispers of warmth in the crisp air,
A gentle touch, beyond compare.

They stretch and reach through leafy trees,
Kissing petals, stirring a breeze,
Illuminating paths where shadows creep,
Awakening dreams from restful sleep.

Joy spills forth in radiant rays,
Chasing darkness, igniting praise,
Each beam a note in Nature's song,
In its warmth, we all belong.

As day unfolds in light's embrace,
Time unfurls, a tender grace,
So let us bask in the sun's sweet gleam,
For life's delights are born from dreams.

Paradise Found in Petals

In gardens vibrant, where blossoms glow,
Whispers of fragrance in soft winds flow,
Each petal's hue, a story told,
A tapestry of love, in colors bold.

Nature's artistry on full display,
A paradise blooms, where heartbeats sway,
From roses' blush to the lily's white,
Every bloom shines, pure delight.

Butterflies flutter, a dance so sweet,
Around the petals, on gentle feet,
In this haven, worries cease,
Among the flowers, we find our peace.

As time drips slowly through petals fair,
We breathe in beauty, beyond compare,
In gardens lush, our souls unwind,
Paradise found, in Nature's mind.

Crescendo of Evening Glow

As day bids farewell in a fiery blaze,
The sky ignites in warm, golden rays,
Crickets sing in the twilight's embrace,
A symphony of night in a timeless space.

Mountains silhouette against the horizon,
Stars awaken, a celestial season,
Soft whispers echo of day's soft end,
In the arms of dusk, new dreams ascend.

Colors blend in a magical swirl,
Night unfurls, as the mysteries whirl,
The moon casts shadows, a gentle glow,
In evening's arms, we all come to know.

With every heartbeat, the world softly sighs,
In the crescendo where the sunset lies,
We gather the dreams that the night bestows,
In the orchestra of twilight, beauty grows.

Days Drenched in Gold

In the shimmer of dawn, a whispering breeze,
Fields awaken, dressed in sunlight's tease.
Golden rays cascade like a gentle embrace,
Nature rejoices in this luminous space.

Children run freely with laughter in tow,
While the flowers tilt, seeking warmth's gentle glow.
Every moment a treasure, each heartbeat a note,
In days drenched in gold, life rises and floats.

The horizon ignites with the colors of dreams,
As the sun dips low, painting rivers with beams.
Each evening a canvas kissed by the light,
Days drenched in gold melt softly to night.

So hold on to these moments, let time linger long,
In the heart of the sun, we all find our song.
For as seasons will change and daylight will wane,
The memories shine bright, like gold in the rain.

Light and Laughter Intertwined

Beneath the broad canvas of a cerulean sky,
Children's laughter melds with the softest sigh.
Sunbeams dance playfully, casting shadows that glow,
In a world where light and joy beautifully flow.

Each moment a spark, igniting the air,
As hopes rise like bubbles, devoid of all care.
Time stretches and bends, wrapped in warmth's gentle hold,
Where heartbeats turn stories, and dreams unfold.

The echoes of giggles bounce off the tall trees,
While petals of flowers sway with the breeze.
With every shared glance and each radiant smile,
Light and laughter entwined make the world worthwhile.

In this tapestry woven with shimmering threads,
Life blossoms in color where happiness spreads.
So cherish these moments, let them forever shine,

Where light and laughter dance, perfectly aligned.

The Symphony of Solstice

At the brink of the solstice, where shadows grow long,
The earth hums a melody, an ancient song.
In twilight's embrace, the fireflies take flight,
Composing a symphony of day into night.

The sun waves goodbye with a fiery descent,
While stars loom above, a celestial event.
Whispers of summer weave through the trees,
As the world holds its breath in a soft, tranquil ease.

Night blankets the meadow, a cloak rich and deep,
While silence becomes music, lulling us to sleep.

The moon, like a maestro, conducts the pale light,

In the symphony of solstice, all hearts feel its might.

So dance in the shadows, rejoice in the glow,
For the cycle of seasons, like time, will bestow.
A rhythm eternal, with every heartbeat defined,
In the symphony of solstice, true magic we find.

Songs of the Starry Night

Beneath a tapestry of shimmering eyes,
The cosmos unfolds under velvet skies.
Whispers of stardust weave tales of delight,
In the silence, they sing through the blanket of night.

Constellations flicker, like dancers in grace,
Mapping the dreams in this vast, sacred space.
Each star a reminder that hope will ignite,
With songs of the cosmos echoing so bright.

The moon bathes the world in a silver embrace,
While shadows take flight in this mystical place.
Melodies linger, carried by breezes,
In the orchestra of night, cold worries it eases.

So gather your dreams, let them soar to the skies,

In the songs of the starry night, where magic lies.

For in every twinkle, a promise takes flight,
Binding hearts to the rhythm of stars shining bright.

Bliss Beneath the Sun

In fields of gold where daisies sway,
The sunlit hours stretch long and free,
Each shadow dances, lingers to play,
A whispered promise of harmony.

Beneath a sky of azure blue,
The warmth wraps round like a gentle hug,
Every moment feels like something new,
As laughter echoes and hearts are snug.

With every breeze, sweet fragrances bloom,
Nature sings softly, a symphony bright,
In this bright world, there's never room
For weary thoughts, just pure delight.

Under the sun's embrace, we spin,
In timeless joy, our spirits soar,
With every heartbeat, we begin
A love affair with life, evermore.

Portraits of a Warm Afternoon

The sun spills gold on the canvas of day,
Each shadow tells tales of time unwound,
A tapestry woven in vibrant array,
The heart of the afternoon, brilliantly found.

Children's laughter dances through the air,
Kites soar high, painting stories in flight,
Where dreams take shape without a single care,
In the arms of warmth, everything feels right.

Old oak trees whisper secrets to the breeze,
Rays flicker softly, a painter's delight,
As petals blush gently, swaying with ease,
In the golden glow, our spirits unite.

With each moment, we find beauty anew,
In the brush of the sun on our skin,
Sketches of life, with wonders that grew,
A warm afternoon where memories begin.

Nature's Loving Embrace

In valleys deep where wildflowers bloom,
A fragrant lullaby cradles the air,
With every heartbeat, the world finds room,
Nature's embrace whispers tender care.

The mountains stand tall, guardians of peace,
While rivers weave tales of journeys untold,
In this sacred space, our worries cease,
As the sun sets low, painting skies gold.

Leaves rustle softly, secrets they share,
Underneath veils of dappled light's grace,
In the stillness of twilight, souls bare,
In nature's arms, we find our place.

Every sunset a promise, every dawn a chance,
To breathe in the magic, to take in the view,
In the heart of the wild, we learn how to dance,
Embraced by nature, forever renewed.

Dappled Light and Dreamscapes

In the forest's heart, where shadows play,
Dappled light weaves through the whispering leaves,
A world painted soft in a dreamlike array,
Where every pathway beckons and cleaves.

Moss carpets the ground, a velvety bed,
As sunlight dapples through branches entwined,
The echo of whispers still lingers ahead,
A symphony sweet, by the wild defined.

The breeze carries laughter of moments once lost,

In the tapestry woven of silence and sighs,
Each step a reminder of paths now embossed,
Created within where imagination flies.

In this sacred realm of fleeting eye-glances,
The heart finds its rhythm, a sweet serenade,
In dappled light's glow, forever it dances,
Where dreams take their form, and wishes are laid.

Swaying Fields of Gold

In a sea of amber waves that dance,
The sun dips low, a fleeting glance,
A gentle breeze whispers through the wheat,
Nature's canvas, painting lives so sweet.

Golden stalks sway to an unseen tune,
Beneath the broad embrace of the afternoon,
Each petal and leaf in harmony plays,
A glimpse of peace in the summer's rays.

Echoes of Long, Lazy Evenings

The sun drapes low, its warmth a sigh,
As shadows stretch and daylight flies,
A gentle hush blankets the land,
Time slows down, life feels so grand.

Whispers of laughter from the nearby stream,
As crickets serenade the twilight dream,
Stars awaken, one by one,
Echoes of magic, the day is done.

The Rhythm of Crickets' Serenade

In the stillness of dusk, a soft refrain,
Crickets compose their nightly gain,
A symphony of chirps, both wild and sweet,
Nature's orchestra finds its beat.

Under a canopy of twinkling light,
Each note dances in the velvet night,
A lullaby for the weary soul,
In the heart of darkness, they make us whole.

Sun-kissed Moments in Time

Golden rays spill over the hills,
Kissing the earth, igniting our wills,
A fleeting glance at life's embrace,
In sun-kissed moments, we find our place.

With laughter hanging in the air,
Memories weave a tapestry rare,
Captured in time, a frame of bliss,
In every heartbeat, there's a sunlit kiss.

Milton Keynes UK
Ingram Content Group UK Ltd.
UKHW020703191024
449793UK00005B/37